365 DAYS of MINDFUL CONTENT

Daily Prompts for Social Media Growth and Connection

Simply Podcastng

JANUARY 2025

Set the Foundation

Define Your Niche: Tailor your content to your expertise (e.g., mindfulness, spirituality, or coaching).

Set Goals: Post 3–5 times weekly.

Optimize Profile: Create a professional bio, use a clear profile photo, and include a link to your podcast or other platforms.

Research Hashtags: Identify 10–15 niche hashtags relevant to your audience.

First Posts: Share introductory and motivational videos to let viewers know your story and mission.

New Beginnings

Day 1
Share your 2025 intention or word of the year

Day 2
Teach a simple 1-minutes meditation

Day 3
What I wish I knew when starting my mindfulness journey

Day 4
React to a trending audio with an inspiring message

Day 5
Share a personal growth book recommendation

Day 6
How to set spiritual goals for the year

Day 7
A guided 1-minute meditation

Day 8
Ask your audience: "What's your biggest intention for 2025?"

Day 9
What does mindfulness mean to me?

Day 10
Share a personal story about a fresh start.

Day 11
Create a grounding practice for winter blues

Day 12
"Why mornings matter for mindfulness."

Day 13
Reaction to a trending motivational sound.

Day 14
"How to forgive yourself and move forward."

Day 15
Share your favorite book on spirituality.

Day 16
Start a "30 Days of Mindfulness" challenge.

Day 17
Quick tutorial: "How to create a vision board."

Day 18
"One thing I'm leaving behind in 2024..."

Day 19
Share a calming affirmation for your followers.

Day 20
Explain the importance of gratitude journaling.

Day 21
"A life lesson I wish I'd learned sooner."

Day 22
Stitch or duet a trending self-improvement video.

Day 23
"How to ground yourself during tough moments."

Day 24
Share your nighttime mindfulness routine.

Day 25
Encourage followers to set their weekly intention.

Day 26
Create a mantra for the week.

Day 27
"Why mindfulness isn't just meditation."

Day 28
Respond to: "What's one thing you're grateful for today?"

Day 29
"The spiritual practice I can't live without."

Day 30
Share a simple yoga pose for relaxation.

Day 31

Reflect on January and share one takeaway.

Monthly Reflection

FEBRUARY 2025

Content Strategy & Trends

Leverage Trends: Use trending audio and hashtags.
Engagement Content: Post duets, stitches, or reaction videos to popular spiritual or mindfulness content.
Create a Series: Start a 3-part mini-series, such as "Mindfulness in 60 Seconds."
Engage With Comments: Respond to every comment on your posts.
Collaborations: Tag or mention similar creators.

Love & Connection

A month to focus on self-love, connection with others, and mindfulness in relationships.

Day 1
"Self-love is the foundation of all love." Share your favorite self-care ritual.

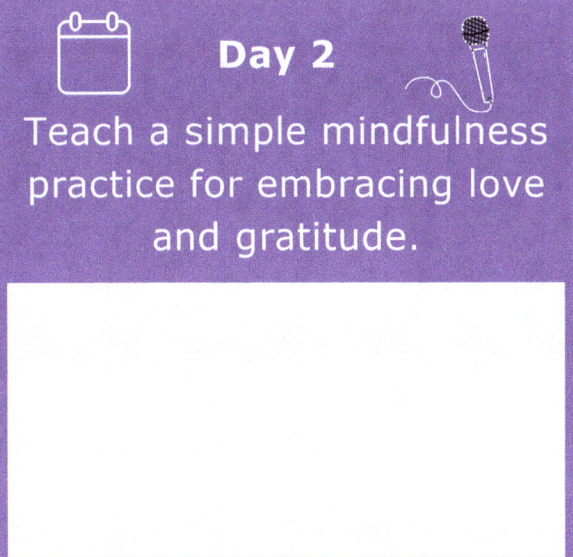

Day 2
Teach a simple mindfulness practice for embracing love and gratitude.

Day 3
"What's one thing you appreciate about yourself today?" Encourage followers to comment.

Day 4
Share a personal story about learning self-compassion.

Day 5
Post a calming video with affirmations for self-love.

Day 6
"How mindfulness strengthens relationships." Share three tips.

Day 7
Ask: "What's one small act of kindness you can do for someone this week?"

Day 8
Create a carousel: "5 Ways to Practice Self-Love This Valentine's Season."

Day 9
Share your favorite quote about love and connection.

Day 10
Guided journaling prompt: "What does love mean to me?"

Day 11
Share a short video of your morning or evening mindfulness routine.

Day 12
"How to be fully present in conversations with loved ones."

Day 13
Reaction video: A trending sound paired with a message of love or kindness.

Day 14
Post a gratitude practice for appreciating the people in your life.

Day 15
"Why self-love isn't selfish."
Share an affirmation.

Day 16
Create a poll: "Do you celebrate Valentine's Day? If yes, how?"

Day 17
Share a mantra for giving and receiving love.

Day 18
Post a calming nature video with affirmations about connection.

Day 19
Teach a breathing practice to cultivate self-compassion.

Day 20
Ask: "What's one thing you've done for yourself this month?"

Day 21
Share a story about a time when mindfulness improved a relationship.

Day 22
Guided meditation: Opening your heart to love and kindness.

Day 23
"How I use mindfulness to navigate feelings of loneliness."

Day 24
Share your favorite book or podcast about love and personal growth.

Day 25
Teach a 5-minute journaling prompt: "What do I love most about my life?"

Day 26
"How mindfulness helps me show up authentically in relationships."

Day 27
Share a calming video with affirmations for inner peace and love.

Day 28
Reflect on February: "One thing I've learned about love and connection this month."

Monthly Reflection

MARCH 2025

Deepen Engagement

Go Live Weekly: Host mindfulness Q&A sessions or guided meditations.
Incorporate Stories: Share personal growth or success stories in 30–60 seconds.
Encourage Follows: End videos with a call to action (e.g., "Follow for daily mindfulness tips!").
Cross-Promote: Share your TikTok on Instagram, Facebook, and Twitter.

Awakening & Growth

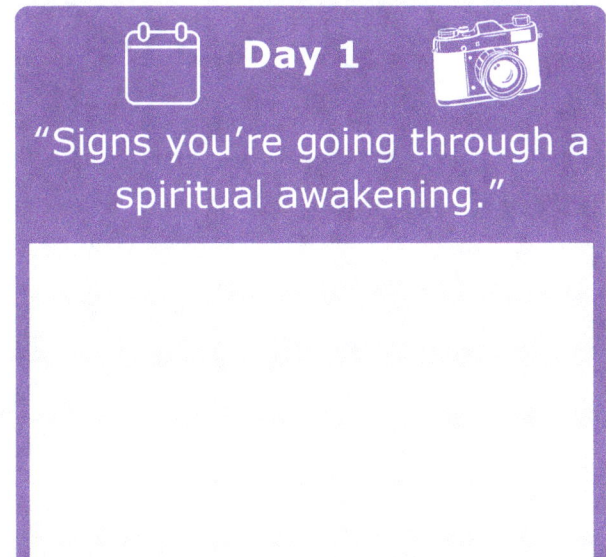

Day 1
"Signs you're going through a spiritual awakening."

Day 2
Share your favorite spring mindfulness activity.

Day 3
Create a video on "How to declutter your mind."

Day 4
Share a spiritual insight that changed your life.

Day 5
Ask: "What's one thing you want to let go of this spring?"

Day 6
Guided meditation for welcoming new beginnings.

Day 7
"A growth lesson I've learned recently."

Day 8
Stitch or duet someone's story about change.

Day 9
Teach a breathing exercise for focus and clarity.

Day 10
"Why spring is the perfect time for reflection."

Day 11
Explain how to use affirmations during transitions.

Day 12
Show a time-lapse of nature with calming affirmations.

Day 13
"How mindfulness has helped me grow."

Day 14
Share a grounding practice for windy March days.

Day 15
Reflect on a personal transformation story.

Day 16
Challenge your followers to spend 5 minutes outdoors.

Day 17
"The spiritual practice I use to embrace change."

Day 18
Show your favorite mindfulness tools (journals, crystals, etc.).

Day 19
"How to practice patience in a fast-paced world."

Day 20
Ask: "What's your favorite way to practice self-care?"

Day 21
Share a mantra for the week.

Day 22
"How I learned to trust the process."

Day 23
A gratitude practice to welcome the season.

Day 24
"A small habit that's transformed my mindfulness."

Day 25
Teach a 5-minute journaling prompt for clarity.

Day 26
Share your favorite spring-themed quote.

Day 27
"How to connect with nature for grounding."

Day 28
Create a "Mindfulness March" 7-day challenge

Day 29
Teach a 5-minute journaling prompt for clarity.

Day 30
Share your favorite spring-themed quote.

Day 31

Preview your plans for April's focus on renewal.

Monthly Reflection

ARPRIL 2025

Experiment & Analyze

Test Formats: Try carousels, memes, and tutorials.
Analytics Review: Use TikTok analytics to identify your best-performing content.
Post More Often: Increase to 5–7 posts weekly based on audience activity.
Engage More: Comment on trending mindfulness or coaching videos.

Renewal & Energy

 Day 1
Guided meditation for renewal and fresh energy.

 **Day 2**
Share a personal story about embracing change.

Day 3
"How to tap into spring energy for mindfulness."

Day 4
Explain the concept of renewal in spirituality.

Day 5
Share your favorite morning ritual for April.

Day 6
Create a "Week of Renewal" challenge for followers.

Day 7
Teach how to create a calming spring altar.

Day 8
"The best advice I've received about starting over."

Day 9
Ask: "What's your favorite way to recharge?"

Day 10
Share a video of blooming flowers with affirmations.

Day 11
"How to forgive yourself and others."

Day 12
Explain the importance of releasing old energy.

Day 13
Share your favorite spiritual tool for grounding.

Day 14
"One thing I'm letting go of this spring…"

Day 15
Create a simple mindfulness challenge: "Do this every morning!"

Day 16
"How to find joy in everyday moments."

Day 17
Share a calming soundtrack or meditation for spring evenings.

Day 18
Reaction video: "Why starting small is powerful."

Day 19
Explain how to reset your energy after burnout.

Day 20
"The importance of embracing imperfections."

Day 21
Show a time-lapse of you practicing mindfulness outdoors.

Day 22
Teach a new journaling prompt: "What do I want to bloom in my life?"

Day 23
Share a story about a time you found clarity.

Day 24
"3 ways to stay present during the busy spring season."

Day 25
Reaction to a trending audio about growth.

Day 26
Share your favorite spiritual podcast or book.

Day 27
"Why mindfulness is a journey, not a destination."

Day 28
Teach how to practice walking meditation.

Day 29
Ask: "What's one thing you want to grow this season?"

Day 30
Reflect on April and share a growth insight.

Monthly Reflection

MAY 2025

Collaborations & Giveaways

Collaborate With Creators: Partner with creators in similar niches for duets, stitches, or shoutouts.
Host a Giveaway: Offer a free coaching session or spiritual guide download for followers.
Promote Podcast: Share snippets of podcast episodes as teasers.

Blossoming & Gratitude

Day 1 — Create a 3-step gratitude practice for mornings.

Day 2 — Share a mindfulness tip for staying balanced.

Day 3
Show your favorite spot for practicing mindfulness.

Day 4
"What mindfulness has taught me about happiness."

Day 5
Reaction: A trending sound paired with a message of gratitude.

Day 6
"Why slowing down helps you move forward."

Day 7
A guided meditation for inner peace.

Day 8
Teach a grounding exercise for warmer days.

Day 9
Share your favorite spring quote about renewal.

Day 10
"How I embrace the energy of May."

Day 11
Share a small, mindful act of kindness.

Day 12
Explain the concept of "being versus doing."

Day 13
Ask: "What's one thing you're grateful for today?"

Day 14
Share a calming video of nature with affirmations.

Day 15
"How to create a gratitude journal in 5 minutes."

Day 16
Talk about a spiritual mentor or lesson that's shaped you.

Day 17
Create a "7 Days of Gratitude" challenge.

Day 18
"How I learned to appreciate the small moments."

Day 19
Ask: "What's blooming in your life this May?"

Day 20
Share an evening ritual for reflection.

Day 21
Reaction to a trending sound: Tie it to mindfulness.

Day 22
"The best advice I've ever received about living in the moment."

Day 23
Create a video showing how you reset your energy mid-day.

Day 24
"Why May feels like a month of possibilities."

Day 25
Teach followers a simple gratitude affirmation.

Day 26
Share a spiritual insight that resonates with the season.

Day 27
"How to remain centered during change."

Day 28
Ask: "What's one thing you've learned this month?"

Day 29
Share a personal story about finding joy.

Day 30
Reflect on May: "What I've learned about gratitude."

Day 31

Preview your June theme of alignment and growth.

Monthly Reflection

JUNE 2025

Seasonal Relevance

Summer Themes: Tie mindfulness to summer activities or vacations.
Storytelling: Create longer, engaging videos about your journey.
Create Challenges: Start a mindfulness challenge for followers.

Alignment & Energy

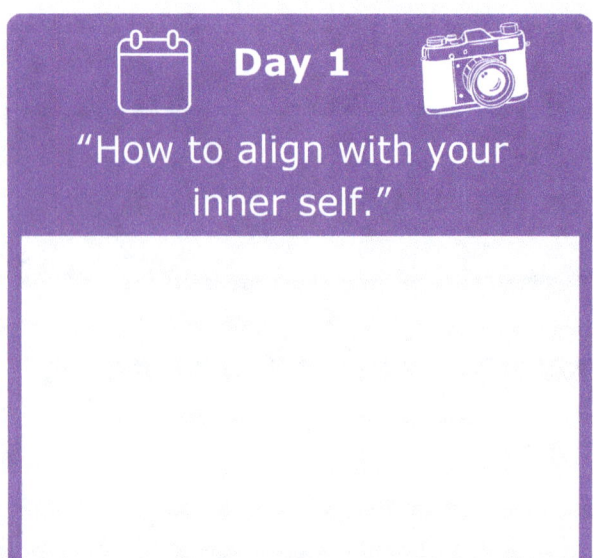

Day 1
"How to align with your inner self."

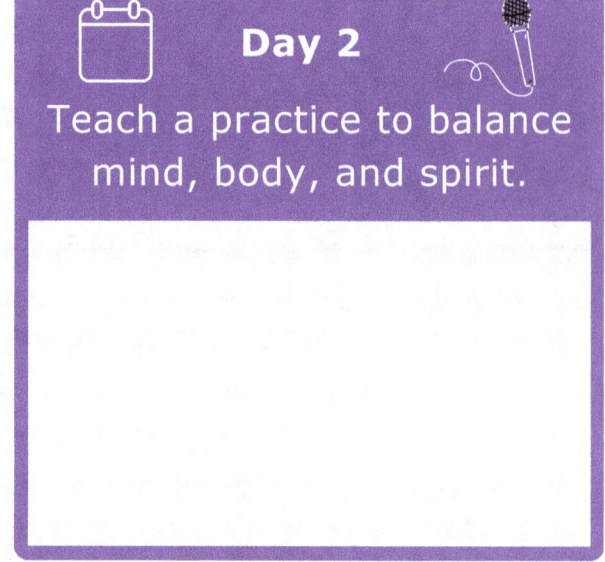

Day 2
Teach a practice to balance mind, body, and spirit.

Day 3
Share a morning routine for summer energy.

Day 4
"Why alignment is key to personal growth."

Day 5
Explain how you set boundaries to protect your energy.

Day 6
Share a story about a time you felt in alignment.

Day 7
"Signs you're out of alignment and how to reset."

Day 8
Guided meditation: Visualizing your aligned self.

Day 9
Teach a mindfulness activity for outdoor adventures.

Day 10
"3 ways to reconnect with purpose."

Day 11
Share a story about a time you felt aligned with your purpose.

Day 12
Reaction video: A trending sound that matches "finding your flow."

Day 13
"How to create a daily routine that aligns with your goals."

Day 14
Share a mindfulness tip for maintaining focus.

Day 15
Ask: "What does alignment mean to you?"

Day 16
Guided meditation: Connecting with your inner self.

Day 17
Share a calming nature video with affirmations about balance.

Day 18
"How to recharge your energy after a busy week."

Day 19
Create a "7 Days to Realignment" challenge.

Day 20
Show a quick breathing practice for instant calm.

Day 21
Share a time you overcame obstacles to realign with your values.

Day 22
Ask: "What's one thing you do to stay centered?"

Day 23
"How to recognize when you're out of alignment."

Day 24
Share a mantra for realignment and focus.

Day 25
Teach a grounding exercise for long summer days.

Day 26
"Why energy management is as important as time management."

Day 27
Share your favorite summer mindfulness book or resource.

Day 28
Show a time-lapse of your favorite calming activity.

Day 29
Reflect on a moment of alignment this month.

Day 30
Share your favorite spring-themed quote.

Monthly Reflection

_____
_____
_____
_____
_____
_____
_____
_____
_____
_____
_____
_____
_____
_____
_____
_____
_____

JULY 2025

Consistency & Scaling

Maintain Posting Frequency: Stick to 5–7 posts per week.
Dive Into Niche Topics: Address specific audience questions in depth.
Repurpose Content: Use snippets from your podcasts or live streams.
Stay Trendy: Continue using popular audios, hashtags, and effects.

Freedom & Reflection

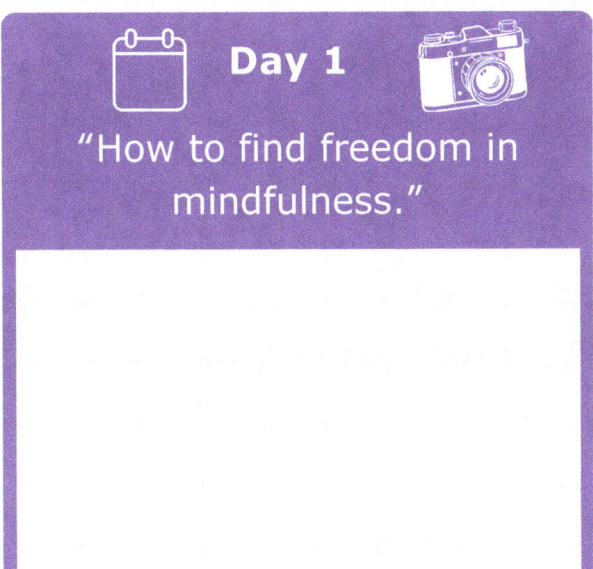

Day 1
"How to find freedom in mindfulness."

Day 2
Share your favorite calming summer activity.

Day 3
Teach a gratitude practice for summer adventures.

Day 4
"Why reflection is powerful during busy times."

Day 5
Ask: "What does freedom mean to you?"

Day 6
Show a mindful moment from your day.

Day 7
"3 simple ways to stay present this summer."

Day 8
Guided meditation for embracing stillness.

Day 9
Share an inspiring story about personal freedom.

Day 10
"How mindfulness helps me overcome stress."

Day 11
Teach a morning intention-setting practice.

Day 12
Ask: "What's your favorite way to recharge in July?"

Day 13
Reaction video: A trending audio about joy or growth.

Day 14
Share a mantra for embracing change.

Day 15
"How to balance productivity with mindfulness."

Day 16
Share a personal story about finding inner peace.

Day 17
Teach a breathing technique to cool down and center.

Day 18
Ask: "What's your favorite summer memory?"

Day 19
Show a time-lapse of nature with calming affirmations.

Day 20
"The importance of living in the moment."

Day 21
Share a spiritual book recommendation for summer.

Day 22
"How to use mindfulness to embrace uncertainty."

Day 23
Create a 5-minute guided journaling session.

Day 24
Create a 5-minute guided journaling session.

Day 25
Share a favorite summer-themed mindfulness tool.

Day 26
"How to create space for yourself in busy times."

Day 27
Teach a simple grounding exercise for outdoor moments.

Day 28
Share a calming nature video and ask: "What brings you peace?"

Day 29
Reflect on July: "What freedom looks like to me now."

Day 30
Preview August: Focus on transformation and abundance.

Day 31

Encourage followers to set intentions for August.

Monthly Reflection

AUGUST 2025

Consistency & Scaling

Maintain Posting Frequency: Stick to 5–7 posts per week.
Dive Into Niche Topics: Address specific audience questions in depth.
Repurpose Content: Use snippets from your podcasts or live streams.
Stay Trendy: Continue using popular audios, hashtags, and effects.

Transformation & Abundance

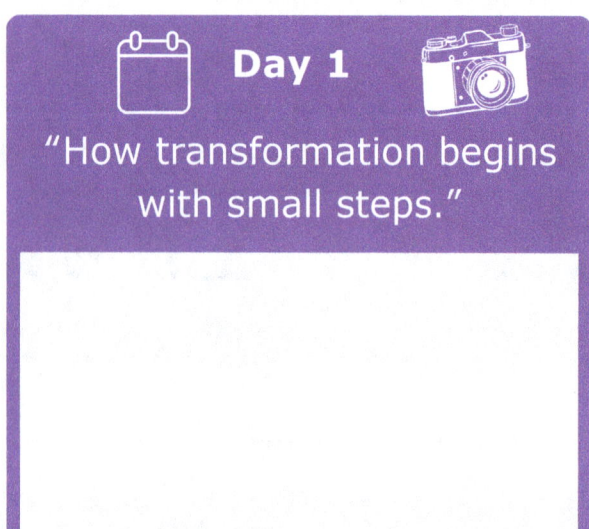

Day 1 — "How transformation begins with small steps."

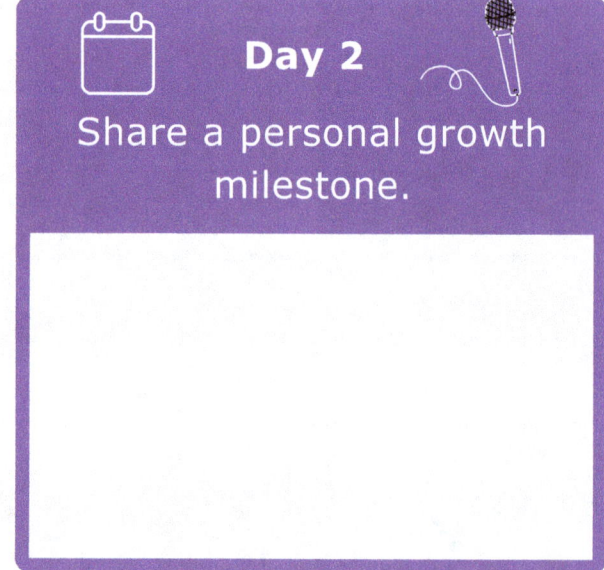

Day 2 — Share a personal growth milestone.

Day 3
Ask: "What's one area in your life you're transforming?"

Day 4
Share your favorite affirmation for abundance.

Day 5
Teach a visualization practice for manifesting abundance.

Day 6
"How I embrace change in my life."

Day 7
Share a spiritual tool or technique for creating abundance.

Day 8
Guided meditation: Tapping into an abundant mindset.

Day 9
"Why letting go is necessary for transformation."

Day 10
Reaction video: A trending sound tied to personal growth.

Day 11
"How mindfulness has shifted my perspective on abundance."

Day 12
Teach a quick journaling prompt: "What am I grateful for today?"

Day 13
Share a calming scene with abundance-themed affirmations.

Day 14
"Why transformation can be uncomfortable but worth it."

Day 15
A morning practice for attracting positivity.

Day 16
"What abundance means to me."

Day 17
Show your evening mindfulness routine for reflection.

Day 18
Teach a technique to release limiting beliefs.

Day 19
"How I stay centered during big changes."

Day 20
Share a story about a transformative moment in your life.

Day 21
Create a "7 Days of Transformation" challenge.

Day 22
Ask: "What's one way you've grown this year?"

Day 23
Share your favorite mindfulness tool for focus.

Day 24
"Why gratitude is the key to abundance."

Day 25
Teach a grounding exercise for new beginnings.

Day 26
Share your favorite August-themed quote.

Day 27
"How I celebrate small wins."

Day 28
Reflect on August: "What abundance looks like to me now."

Day 29
Preview September: Focus on balance and renewal.

Day 30
Share a quick breathing practice to end the month strong.

Day 31

Ask: "What's one lesson you've learned this month?"

Monthly Reflection

SEPTEMBER 2025

Consistency & Scaling

Maintain Posting Frequency: Stick to 5–7 posts per week.
Dive Into Niche Topics: Address specific audience questions in depth.
Repurpose Content: Use snippets from your podcasts or live streams.
Stay Trendy: Continue using popular audios, hashtags, and effects.

Balance & Renewal

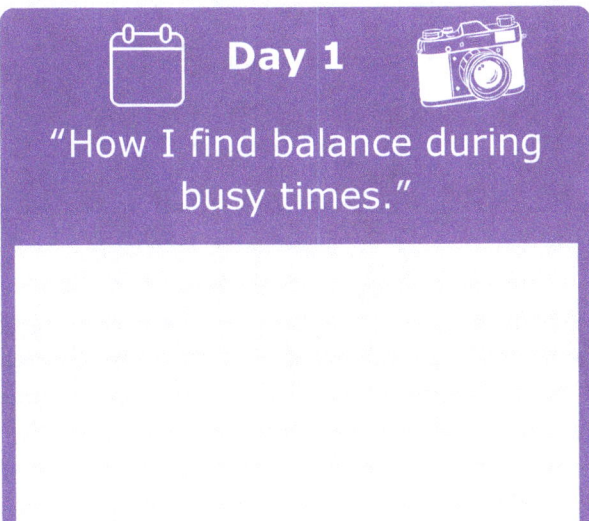

Day 1
"How I find balance during busy times."

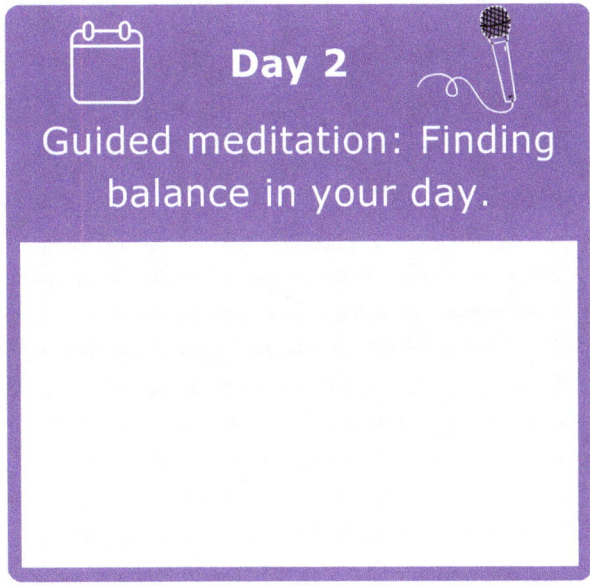

Day 2
Guided meditation: Finding balance in your day.

Day 3
Share a personal story about seeking renewal.

Day 4
"3 ways to stay grounded during transitions."

Day 5
Reaction video: Use a calming, seasonal sound.

Day 6
"How I reset my energy for fall."

Day 7
Share a mindfulness tool for balance.

Day 8
Teach a 5-minute journaling prompt: "Where can I find more balance?"

Day 9
"Why balance is about alignment, not perfection."

Day 10
Ask: "What does balance look like in your life?"

Day 11
"How mindfulness helps me navigate change."

Day 12
Guided journaling prompt: "What areas of my life need more balance?"

Day 13
Share a personal story about finding renewal.

Day 14
Teach a grounding technique for seasonal shifts.

Day 15
Ask: "What does renewal mean to you this fall?"

Day 16
"Why balance is about progress, not perfection."

Day 17
Share a simple mindfulness practice for busy schedules.

Day 18
Reaction to a trending video: Add your thoughts on balance.

Day 19
Create a fall-inspired gratitude practice.

Day 20
"How to release what no longer serves you."

Day 21
Show your morning mindfulness routine for a balanced start.

Day 22
Share a mantra for embracing change this season.

Day 23
"How to stay present when life feels overwhelming."

Day 24
Guided meditation: Letting go of stress and welcoming renewal.

Day 25
Share your favorite quote about balance.

Day 26
Ask: "What's one way you're prioritizing yourself this fall?"

Day 27
"Why mindfulness is essential during transitions."

Day 28
Teach a 3-step evening routine to reflect and renew.

Day 29
Share a nature video with affirmations for balance.

Day 30
Reflect on September: "What balance has taught me this month."

Monthly Reflection

OCTOBER 2025

Finishing Strong

Reflect on Progress: Evaluate what's worked and tweak the plan.
Festive Content: Relate mindfulness practices to holidays and year-end reflections.
Push for Community: Create polls, respond to DMs, and build a stronger bond with followers.
Plan for 2026: Start thinking about long-term growth strategies.

- **Additional Tips:**

Video Quality: Ensure clear visuals and sound.
Authenticity: Be genuine and relatable.
Stay Updated: Follow trends and algorithm changes.

Reflection & Introspection

Day 1
"Why fall is the perfect season for introspection."

Day 2
Share a morning ritual for grounding in autumn energy.

Day 3
Teach a simple journaling prompt: "What lessons have I learned this year?"

Day 4
"How to use mindfulness to navigate transitions."

Day 5
Share a calming video of fall leaves with affirmations.

Day 6
Guided meditation: Reflecting on the year so far.

Day 7
Share your favorite autumn-inspired quote.

Day 8
"3 ways to cultivate gratitude during autumn."

Day 9
Ask: "What's one thing you're reflecting on this month?"

Day 10
"Why letting go is essential for new beginnings."

Day 11
Teach a practice for releasing negative energy.

Day 12
Share a story about a pivotal moment of introspection.

Day 13
Guided meditation: Connecting with your inner self.

Day 14
Reaction to a trending sound about change or growth.

Day 15
"How I embrace the beauty of slowing down."

Day 16
Create a "7 Days of Reflection" challenge.

Day 17
"What mindfulness has taught me about the power of pause."

Day 18
Ask: "What's your favorite mindful moment in autumn?"

Day 19
Share a spiritual book or podcast recommendation for fall.

Day 20
"How to stay present during moments of uncertainty."

Day 21
Share a calming video of your favorite fall activity.

Day 22
"Why self-compassion is vital during times of change."

Day 23
Guided journaling: "What am I most grateful for right now?"

Day 24
"How mindfulness helps me embrace the seasons of life."

Day 25
Share a mantra for finding balance in October.

Day 26
Reflect on how you've grown this month and invite followers to do the same.

Day 27
Teach a grounding exercise for cooler days.

Day 28
"How to embrace the present moment when life feels overwhelming."

Day 29
Share your evening routine for reflection and renewal.

Day 30
Reflect on October: "What introspection has taught me this month."

Day 31

Preview November: Focus on gratitude and connection.

Monthly Reflection

NOVEMBER 2025

Finishing Strong

Reflect on Progress: Evaluate what's worked and tweak the plan.
Festive Content: Relate mindfulness practices to holidays and year-end reflections.
Push for Community: Create polls, respond to DMs, and build a stronger bond with followers.
Plan for 2026: Start thinking about long-term growth strategies.

- **Additional Tips:**

Video Quality: Ensure clear visuals and sound.
Authenticity: Be genuine and relatable.
Stay Updated: Follow trends and algorithm changes.

Gratitude & Connection

Day 1
"What I'm most grateful for as the year winds down."

Day 2
Share a personal story about gratitude.

Day 3
Teach a 5-minute gratitude journaling practice.

Day 4
"Why connection is essential for a mindful life."

Day 5
Share your favorite gratitude affirmation.

Day 6
Guided meditation: Cultivating gratitude and connection.

Day 7
Ask: "What's one thing you're grateful for today?"

Day 8
Share a calming nature video with gratitude-themed affirmations.

Day 9
"How mindfulness helps me nurture meaningful connections."

Day 10
Create a "Week of Gratitude" challenge for your followers.

Day 11
Share your favorite quote about the power of gratitude.

Day 12
"How to make gratitude a daily habit."

Day 13
Reaction video: A trending sound paired with a message of connection.

Day 14
"What I've learned about gratitude this year."

Day 15
Teach a simple breathing exercise to center and connect.

Day 16
Share a personal story about reconnecting with someone.

Day 17
"Why gratitude is the key to abundance."

Day 18
Guided journaling: "Who or what do I want to thank today?"

Day 19
Share a mantra for nurturing connection.

Day 20
"How to stay present and connected during holiday stress."

Day 21
Share a calming video of a cozy fall scene.

Day 22
"Why mindfulness makes the holidays more meaningful."

Day 23
Teach a quick meditation for holiday stress relief.

Day 24
Reflect on a meaningful connection you've nurtured this year.

Day 25
Share your favorite quote about love and connection.

Day 26
Ask: "What's one thing you're most grateful for this season?"

Day 27
Create a video showing how you practice gratitude daily.

Day 28
Guided meditation: Sending gratitude and love to others.

Day 29
Reflect on November: "What connection and gratitude mean to me."

Day 30
Preview December: Focus on reflection and celebration.

Monthly Reflection

_____
_____
_____
_____
_____
_____
_____
_____
_____
_____
_____
_____
_____
_____
_____
_____
_____

DECEMBER 2025

Finishing Strong

Reflect on Progress: Evaluate what's worked and tweak the plan.
Festive Content: Relate mindfulness practices to holidays and year-end reflections.
Push for Community: Create polls, respond to DMs, and build a stronger bond with followers.
Plan for 2026: Start thinking about long-term growth strategies.

- **Additional Tips:**

Video Quality: Ensure clear visuals and sound.
Authenticity: Be genuine and relatable.
Stay Updated: Follow trends and algorithm changes.

Reflection & Celebration

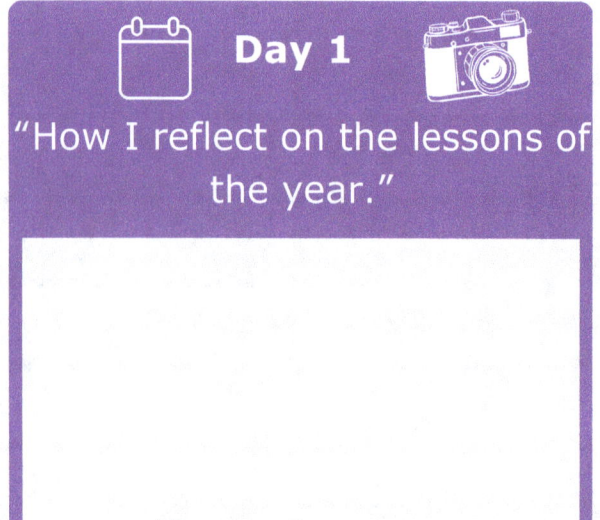

Day 1
"How I reflect on the lessons of the year."

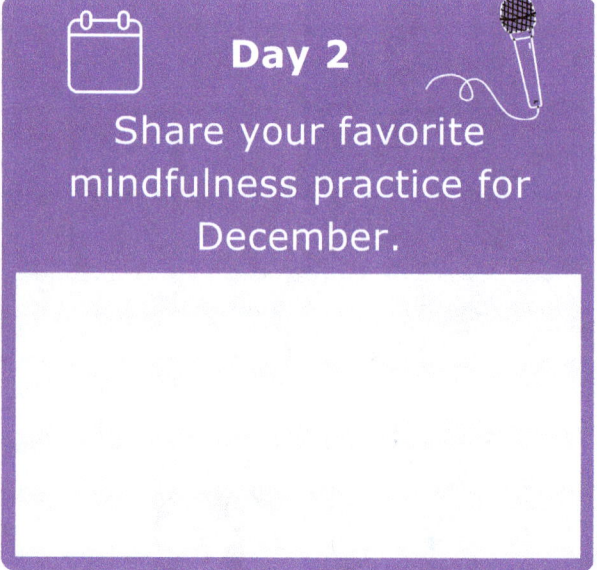

Day 2
Share your favorite mindfulness practice for December.

Day 3
Teach a journaling prompt: "What am I most proud of this year?"

Day 4
Guided meditation: Reflecting on 2025's growth.

Day 5
"How to celebrate small wins mindfully."

Day 6
Share your favorite holiday tradition with a mindfulness twist.

Day 7
"Why reflection is the key to moving forward."

Day 8
Share a personal story about a meaningful moment in 2025.

Day 9
Teach a gratitude practice to close out the year.

Day 10
Ask: "What's one lesson you've learned in 2025?"

Day 11
Share a calming video with year-end affirmations.

Day 12
Create a "Week of Reflection" challenge for followers.

Day 13
Reaction video: A trending sound tied to celebration or gratitude.

Day 14
Share a mantra for letting go of the past.

Day 15

"How I prepare my mindset for a new year."

Day 16

Guided journaling: "What am I letting go of as the year ends?"

Day 17

Share your favorite quote about new beginnings.

Day 18

"How mindfulness has shaped my year."

Day 19
Teach a practice for setting intentions for the new year.

Day 20
Ask: "What's one thing you're celebrating about yourself this year?"

Day 21
"How to bring mindfulness into your holiday celebrations."

Day 22
Share your evening routine for reflecting on the year.

Day 23
Guided meditation: Welcoming the energy of 2026.

Day 24
"Why mindfulness is the greatest gift you can give yourself."

Day 25
Share a calming video with affirmations for joy and peace.

Day 26
"What I've learned about growth and mindfulness in 2025."

Day 27
Teach a breathing practice to ground yourself before the new year.

Day 28
Share a personal reflection: "One thing I'm proud of this year."

Day 29
"How I use mindfulness to create meaningful goals."

Day 30
Reflect on December: "What celebration and reflection mean to me."

Day 31

Celebrate with your audience: "Thank you for joining me in 2025—here's to 2026!"

Monthly Reflection

NOTES

NOTES

NOTES

Struggling to find the perfect idea for your next post? Feeling uninspired or overwhelmed by the pressure to stay consistent on social media?

This workbook is your ultimate solution.

Designed for content creators, entrepreneurs, and mindful influencers, "365 Days of Mindful Content" provides you with a year's worth of thoughtful, engaging, and purposeful prompts to elevate your social media game.

Each prompt is carefully crafted to help you:
✨ Spark meaningful conversations with your audience.
✨ Stay authentic while growing your brand.
✨ Create posts that inspire, connect, and convert.

Whether you're sharing personal stories, teaching valuable lessons, or simply looking to spread positivity, this guide ensures you'll never run out of ideas. From daily reflections to seasonal themes, every page is packed with inspiration to keep your content fresh and aligned with your unique voice.

📖 Your journey to consistent, mindful, and impactful social media starts here.

Perfect for TikTok, Instagram, YouTube, and beyond—this is more than a workbook. It's a tool to unlock your creativity and transform your social media presence.
Let's make every day a post-worthy moment.

www.ingramcontent.com/pod-product-compliance
Lightning Source LLC
Chambersburg PA
CBHW062110220526
45471CB00010B/3679